ETIQUETTE

for Second Marriages

WEDDING ETIQUETTE

for Second Marriages

JO PACKHAM

A STERLING/CHAPELLE BOOK
Sterling Publishing Co. Inc. New York

Library of Congress Cataloging-in-Publication Data

Packham, Jo

Wedding etiquette for second marriages / by Jo Packham.

p. cm.

"A Sterling/Chapelle book."

Includes index.

ISBN 0-8069-0836-X

1. Wedding etiquette. 2. Remarriage. I. Title.

BJ2065.R44P37 1994

395'.22—dc 20 94-27200

CIP

10 9 8 7 6 5 4 3 2 1

A Sterling/Chapelle Book

Published by Sterling Publishing Company, Inc.

387 Park Avenue South, New York, N.Y. 10016

Distributed in Canada by Sterling Publishing

℅ Canadian Manda Group, P.O. Box 920, Station U

Toronto, Ontario, Canada M8Z 5P9

Distributed in Great Britain and Europe by Cassell PLC

Villiers House, 41/47 Strand, London WC2N 5JE, England

Distributed in Australia by Capricorn Link (Australia) Pty Ltd.

P.O. Box 6651, Baulkham Hills, Business Center, NSW 2153, Australia

Printed and bound in Hong Kong

Sterling ISBN 0-8069-0836-X

CONTENTS

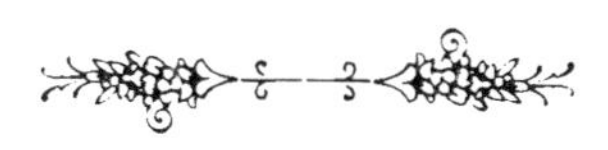

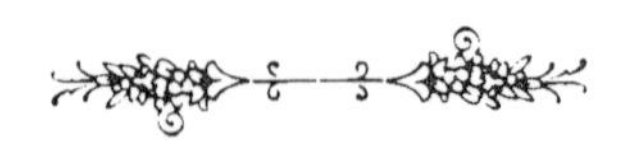

For Ryne:
Whose happiness I wish for more than any other—

Four minds with but a single thought,
Four hearts that beat as only one,
Four souls which love eternal sought,
Were joined before the day was done.

With hope bestowed by a white winged dove
And love's young dreams to guide their way
They vowed for each eternal love
This family . . . God hath joined that day.

Your loving friend,
Jo

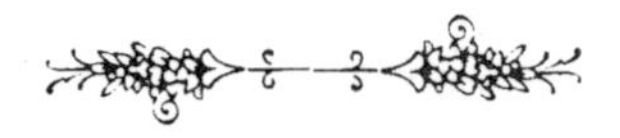

INTRODUCTION

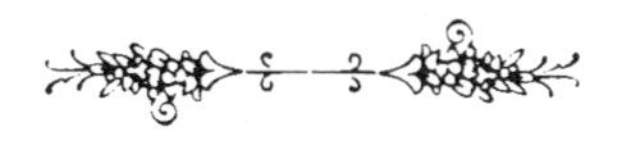

Accepting his proposal, becoming a blushing bride-to-be, and planning a wedding will prove to be one of the most exciting times of your life. It is a time filled with doubt, with emotion, and with expectations that are based predominately, not on reality, but on childhood dreams. That is true even if this is a second marriage for both or either one of you. This time, however, this new love that is being shared is now surrounded by a reality and a set of challenges even more intense than the first time they were faced.

This new set of challenges is very real and can be a reason for concern for all involved, but must never be allowed to cause you to lose your perspective. After all, second marriages, whether yours, his, or both, should be viewed as a special celebration of new hope that is accompanied by a unique and wiser understanding. This is an event that should be as exciting, as memorable, and possibly more rewarding and longer lasting than the first.

"How do I write the engagement announcement? What is the appropriate wording for the wedding invitations? What color wedding dress will I wear? Who will pay for what in regard to the reception?"

For the bride and the groom who are planning their second marriage, these are only a few of dozens of confusing questions that need to be answered. Wedding traditions and details are complicated enough, but when divorces, stepchildren, and other extenuating circumstances are involved, an entirely new set of guidelines and considerations are in order. This book is intended as a source of reference for every bride facing either her, the groom's, or both of their second marriages. It is only a place to begin, a place to help you make your own decisions for what is best for you, the groom, and the significant others that are involved in your wedding plans. It is not intended to serve as a strict set of rules—they simply do not exist!

THE PROPOSAL

Proposing, for the groom, should be considered no less important for a second marriage than it was for the first. The proposal should not be any less romantic now that the groom is older and this is either his second or your second proposal. It will still be a fairy-tale moment for you. It will be the magic question that causes the fantasy to become reality and the occasion that holds the hope that promises will be kept. Now with the uttering of four simple words, the transformation from being simply a woman in love into a new bride begins to take place.

THE RING

After the groom or the two of you decide that you definitely should get married, one of the first decisions will be what kind of rings to give. Here again, the fact that this is a second marriage should have no influence on the selection of these gifts. The rings that are chosen may be as ornate or as simple, as large or as small, as your style and dreams dictate. It will still need to be decided if there will be an engagement ring or simply a wedding band. Other considerations include whether you will both wear rings or whether only you will, whether the rings will be new or family heirlooms, and whether you will help select the stone and setting or whether he will decide to surprise you with his choice.

The possibility always exists for more than one misunderstanding to occur when the subject of engagement rings and wedding bands is being considered. Whatever is decided, it would be wise for the two of you to discuss the subject of rings openly and honestly, preferably before the ring is presented, or immediately after if it is to be a surprise. This, too, is a moment that should be filled with as much love and as many memories as it was the first time.

The decision on what should be done with wedding rings from a first marriage should be discussed between you and your fiancé. If the engagement ring is valuable, it may be kept for a daughter or for a son to give to his new bride. If your fiancé has no objections, you may choose to have it reset into a dinner ring, a pendant, or a broach. It is unnecessary to store an expensive piece of jewelry such as this unless it evokes painful memories or elicits uncomfortable feelings from your fiancé, in which case you may choose to sell the ring or rings.

ANNOUNCING YOUR ENGAGEMENT

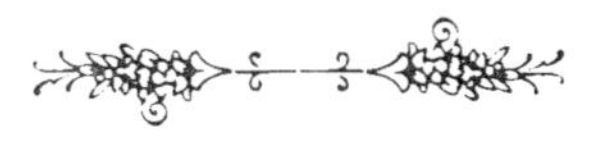

Regardless of how or when it happens, becoming engaged stirs a whirlwind of emotions that brings daydreams into the realm of reality and sends you spinning into a future filled with hopes and romantic expectations. Once the news is out that you are going to be married, parties and plans and the delightful feeling of being the bride are what you have to look forward to, even if this is the second engagement for either or both of you.

Becoming engaged is the first link in this new and exciting chain of events and announcing your engagement is link number two. Traditionally with first marriages, the two of you would go to your parents first, announce the engagement, and ask for their blessing. After informing your parents of your engagement, the two of you would personally visit the groom's parents and make the same announcement. With second engagements, if there are children involved from previous marriages, you will want to change the tradition and tell them of the engagement first. This is probably best handled on a one-on-one basis. This allows each child the opportunity to openly express his or her feelings, which will be many and varied. Before either you or the groom make any announcement to either your children or the groom's children, the two of you should discuss how the children will be involved in the wedding festivities themselves. Letting them know from the very first minute that they are very important in your new relationship and that they will play a major role in the upcoming events will help them feel important, wanted, and needed. If, however, they seem reluctant to participate, do not press the issue. Time and the upcoming events may change their minds naturally.

After the announcement has been made to the children and they have had a sufficient amount of time to adjust to this new set of circumstances, a meeting should be planned with everyone—you, the children, and your fiancé. Any worries should be addressed and plans that include everyone should begin. After this meeting, you and the groom should decide together how to announce the engagement to your parents and to his parents. You may choose to follow tradition or you may choose to have an engagement party. If you opt for a party for family and friends, before everyone is invited it may be wise for you to personally inform your ex-spouse of your new plans immediately after telling the children and both sets of parents. This may or may not be a good time to discuss the changes your upcoming marriage will cause for all of you. If your relationship is an amicable one, your ex-partner can help alleviate some of the children's fears. If your relationship is less than friendly, you will have to deal with the announcement and your future plans in a manner that you feel is best for everyone involved. This is also true if the situation applies to the groom and his ex-spouse.

Announcing your engagement to other family and friends can be as simple or as festive as the two of you wish it to be. Whatever you choose to do is appropriate.

If you wish to announce your engagement simply, you will want to notify family and friends immediately after the children, both sets of parents, and ex-spouses. The announcement can be made in person, or it can be made by means of a telephone call or a handwritten note for friends and family who live too far for you to travel to tell them the news in person.

On the other hand, if there were no special events attached to the announcement of your first marriage, you may choose to have an engagement party to announce your second marriage. The engagement party, which will probably be the first of many celebrations, traditionally takes place after you have told immediate family and friends of your engagement and upcoming marriage, but before the announcement appears in the newspapers. For first marriages, six months to one year from the time of the announcement to the wedding date is the norm; for second marriages, it may be shorter.

Engagement Party

If you choose to have an engagement party, you will probably break the tradition of having the party hosted by your parents and host the party yourselves. The two of you will need to decide who should be invited and whether the announcement is to be a surprise. You may choose to surprise everyone except the children from the previous marriages. Depending on their ages and inexperience, this could be unfair to them. They should be invited to the party, but should be informed of its purpose beforehand.

If you are a bride who loves tradition, you will want to proceed with the same traditions as if this were your first wedding. Your engagement ring is usually your fiancé's engagement gift to you. You do not have to give him a gift, but if you choose to do so, the engagement party may be the perfect time to present him with it. The gift you choose should be something personal and lasting. It is a nice idea to include engagement gifts for the children of first marriages as well. It helps bring them into the festivities and makes them feel very important. After all, if there are children involved, both partners are becoming "engaged" to the children as well.

Your engagement party can be a formal affair, a western barbecue, or a wine and cheese party. If the party is very formal, engraved invitations are issued. If engraved invitations are issued, it is practically a promise that a large formal wedding will follow. If the engagement party is to be less formal, handwritten notes, purchased invitations, or telephone calls are suitable. Invitations to engagement parties do not necessarily mention the reason for the party. They are sent in the name of the person or persons who are announcing the engagement (here the children's name could be included) and hosting the party. They are sent to guests who include your family and friends, the wedding party, the groom's parents, and their family and friends. It is nice if each of the children are asked to include one or two friends of their own on the list so that they will have someone to associate with at the party as well. Whether or not to invite step families is something that should be considered carefully. Generally invitations are not sent to guests who will not be invited to the wedding.

However large or small, formal or informal, your engagement party is, remember that you and your fiancé are the guests of honor. This is a very special occasion that officially makes your intentions public, gives all of those close to you the opportunity to offer their congratulations and best wishes, and allows friends and families to become acquainted. Make certain that, as the guests of honor, you and the groom make all of the necessary introductions. Often, it is best to procure everyone's attention at a specific time early in the evening (or at the beginning of the dinner if a meal is being served), when you and the groom—and the children, if they have invited guests—will introduce everyone. You will want to give their name and their association to either or both of you.

At this time, with guests assembled and their attention procured, the father of the bride traditionally proposes a toast to his daughter and her fiancé. However, if you have a son who is old enough, you may wish to have him propose the first toast. If you are both older and you feel more comfortable, you may wish for a male friend of either yours or the groom to propose the toast. Everyone, except you and the groom, raise their glasses and drink. The groom-to-be answers with a toast and a short speech to the bride, to your children, and, if appropriate, to your family. When he is finished, other toasts may follow.

Newspaper Announcements

At this point, you may choose to announce your engagement officially by placing a notice in the newspaper. After you have decided on a wedding date, this can be done as soon as possible. The decision to make such an announcement should be agreed upon by you and your fiancé. Many betrothed feel uncomfortable announcing a second marriage, but many do not. Most second marriage announcements appear in the paper not more than one month before the day of the wedding. If your second marriage follows closely behind the end of the first marriage, you may wish to announce the wedding only and not the engagement.

If you are a young divorcé, you may choose to have your parents announce your second wedding using your former husband's last name if you have continued to use his name or your maiden name if you had your name changed back following the divorce. This may read as follows:

Mr. and Mrs. Randal Christensen announce the engagement of their daughter, Mrs. Jennifer Hollingsworth, (or Jennifer Ann Hollingsworth) (or Jennifer Ann Christensen) to . . .

If you are older, you may announce your own engagement in the following manner:

The engagement of Ms. Jennifer Ann Hollingsworth to Mr. Barry M. Davis has been announced . . .

You may then choose to include in your announcement whatever information you feel is important. For example:

- ♥ Schools attended and any degrees received.
- ♥ Current places of employment and job titles for both of you.
- ♥ The date and location (month and city) of the wedding ceremony and reception.

If you do elect to make an official newspaper announcement, and if you or your fiancé are from different towns, you may choose to have the announcement appear in several different cities' papers.

Every newspaper has its own policy and special requirements for printing announcements. You will need to inquire as to any specifics, in addition to deadlines and fees. Check with the life-style editor of each individual newspaper as to its guidelines.

WEDDING ATTENDANTS

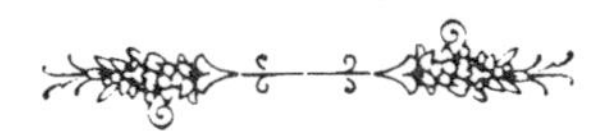

Making and enjoying memories is one of the treasures you share with friends. That is why the selection of who is to be in your wedding with you and your fiancé is so important.

Asking someone to be a wedding participant is not only an ancient custom, but an honor and a great responsibility. In the past, there were definite rules about whom should be included, absolute guidelines on what their roles should be, and every member of the wedding party had a well-defined area of responsibility. Today, however, with the change in life-styles and attitudes, it is up to you and your fiancé to decide what is best for the two of you, your families, and your wedding participants.

When considering who to select as part of your supporting cast for this marriage, you must first decide what style of wedding you are going to have. Even though this is your second marriage, will it be formal and very traditional? Will it follow an informal, contemporary theme such as a western barbecue? Will it be somewhere in between? Your decision will dictate, to a certain extent, the number of attendants you will select and possibly who they will be.

You will want to include family and friends in your wedding party, and you will want to make the selections with great care so as not to hurt anyone's feelings. Because this is a marriage that may include children from previous marriages, you will definitely want to include them in the wedding party. Depending on their ages, daughters can participate in every way from flower girl to maid-of-honor; sons can be ring bearers, best man, or even give you away (my son from my first marriage gave me away—he was eleven and it was a moment I will never forget!) I cannot stress enough how important I believe it is to give the children an important role in the wedding. After all, you are marrying each others' entire immediate family—not just each other!

Remember that not everyone is aware of his or her responsibilities—especially if they are young or if they have never participated in a wedding before. Individual responsibilities are even more unclear in second marriages. Do not assume that they know what is expected of them, and do not hesitate to talk to them about their duties and responsibilities and your expectations. Never expect more of your wedding party than they can reasonably afford to give—both in time and financial considerations. You want your wedding to be as memorable for your participants as you do for you and the groom.

The Honor Attendant

The honor attendant has one of the most important roles in the wedding. She will help you in every way needed during the preparations for the wedding and throughout the actual festivities. You will need to select that perfect someone whom you are closer to than any other and someone you can depend upon and trust to be responsible and diligent in her duties.

The maid- or matron- (if she is married) of-honor traditionally is a sister, a family member, or a very close friend who is approximately your age. In the case of a second marriage, she may be a daughter, a stepdaughter, or your mother.

Traditionally, only one person is selected to be a maid- or matron-of-honor, but for a second marriage, you may elect to have two. You may have a married family member or friend who is your age or older become your matron-of-honor, while a daughter may become your maid-of-honor.

The Best Man

The best man was historically the groom's brother or closest friend. Today, especially if this is the groom's second marriage, he may choose his son, your son, or his father. Next to you and the groom, the best man shares with your honor attendant the distinction of being the most important member of the wedding party. His duties are many and his responsibilities important for he is to relieve the groom of as many details and as much responsibility as possible. If there is no wedding coordinator, the best man and the maid- or matron-of-honor are responsible for making certain that the ceremony and reception go exactly as planned. He is the one who should be prepared for and handle any emergency! He, therefore, should be the relative or friend the groom selects over any other, not only because he is the closest, but because he is the most responsible and dependable and has the best sense of humor!

In the case of second marriages, if you or the groom feel it is most important to have a son act as best man even though he is simply too young to handle so much responsibility, then you will want to consider having more than one best man or assigning the majority of the best man's responsibilities to the head usher.

Bridesmaids & Groomsmen

You have decided to marry, discussed and established a budget, chosen a wedding style, and selected your honor attendant and best man. Now the two of you should think about how many attendants each of you will have and who they will be. You will need to be selective, consider the feelings of family and friends, begin with traditional guidelines, and then modify them to fit your own personal needs.

Traditionally, a groomsman was selected by the groom as an escort for a bridesmaid and an usher was at the wedding strictly to seat guests before the ceremony. The rule of thumb was to have one usher for every fifty guests, assuming that one-half to three-fourths of your invited guests will attend. In today's society, however, the roles are combined, the terms are used interchangeably, and there may be any number you and the groom desire.

The groom may choose to have one groomsman for each of your bridesmaids and then ask additional individuals to be ushers, naming one the head usher. Another option is to have all groomsmen serve as ushers, seating guests before the ceremony and joining the wedding party shortly before the ceremony.

Child Attendants

Young children can add a great deal of charm to wedding festivities and, because this is your second marriage, it may be essential that they are included in all phases of the activities. Due to their unpredictability, you may elect to include no more than two child attendants. It is, however, a decision that you and the groom should make, depending on how many young children you want to have involved and how much help you can solicit to keep them supervised and entertained.

Child attendants are usually between four and eight years of age. If you elect to have attendants between these ages participate, or children even younger than four years old, you will need to make some alternate plans. Make certain that you have invited the children to all pre-wedding festivities, do not give any child attendant a task where there could be problems if the task remains uncompleted, and make certain that you have appointed someone who is not involved in the wedding festivities to closely supervise them. You do not want that responsibility to remain with you or the groom, even if they are your children.

Flower Girl & Ring Bearer

Nothing is more delightful than a young girl dressed in wedding finery—especially if she is your very own! She may walk alone or with the ring bearer, but she always comes immediately before you and whomever is escorting you down the aisle.

The ring bearer is traditionally a boy, but as a contemporary bride at her second wedding, if between you and the groom there are two daughters, you may have one of them be a ring bearer and one a flower girl.

In the recessional, the flower girl is escorted by the ring bearer and they both follow immediately behind you and the groom. In special circumstances, if both the flower girl and the ring bearer are yours or the groom's children, you may have them walk down the aisle on either side of you if there is room, or you may choose to have them walk in front of you as the youngest representatives of this new family.

Family Members

Your wedding, whether it be your first or your second, is a memorable and momentous occasion for your parents as well as for you. It is a time when you can become even closer to them by involving them in as many aspects of the wedding plans as you and the groom feel comfortable. It is also a perfect time to become closer to the groom's parents—they will probably love to be involved as well.

Remember, however, that their feelings are as varied as yours—the range goes from the exhilaration of seeing you so happy and full of hope for the future, to the hesitation that is caused by the circumstances that brought about a second marriage. Be careful of their feelings, be considerate of their suggestions, and be confident of the fact that their offers of advice and involvement are meant to help and make you happy.

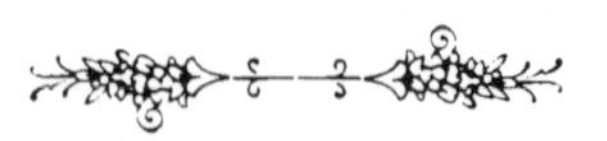

"Few things are more pleasing to see than a grateful heart wrapped up in the people you love. It is a pleasure to be with them; a joy to do things for them!"

—Adapted from Winnifred C. Jardine

PARTIES, SHOWERS & DINNERS

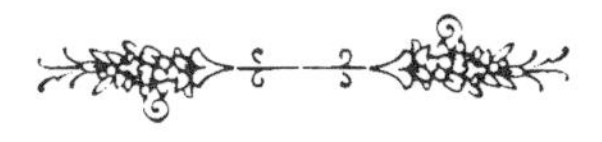

Tradition has it that the first bridal shower took place in Holland when a maiden fell in love with a poor miller. Her father forbade the marriage, denying her the customary bridal dowry. So the miller's friends decided to help the young couple and "showered" the bride with gifts. Today, bridal showers are very different from those steeped in tradition that were given for our mothers and grandmothers. Even though you have been married before, it is still perfectly appropriate for you to be honored now by relatives and friends. Your upcoming marriage may be celebrated at anything from a picnic on the banks of the river to an elegant dinner for couples with wine and romantic music. You may share your new dreams with just your female friends at a quiet afternoon tea or you and your fiancé, sometimes with and sometimes without the children, may be given a party—maybe at an amusement park which would be great fun for everyone invited regardless of age!

Occasionally a bride and groom, being married for the second time, are financially settled enough that when friends and family wish to give them a party, they request "no gifts" be put on the invitation.

The Bridesmaids' Luncheon

This is the perfect time to say thank you to those friends who have helped and shared so much in the preparation and memories of your wedding day. After all, "a true friend is the greatest of all blessings."

This party is traditionally given by you or your mother, but it is becoming more acceptable for the groom's mother, a female relative, or a close friend to act as hostess.

A large bridesmaids' party, which is as acceptable for second marriages as it is for firsts, includes you, your attendants, the flower girl, the hostess, both mothers, sisters and sisters-in-law of both you and the groom, and any female relatives or friends you wish to include. A smaller party would include only you, your attendants, the flower girl, the two mothers, and the hostess.

Traditionally, the bridesmaids' party was a luncheon that was scheduled the day of the wedding. It is becoming more popular, however, to hold these festivities sometime within the week of the wedding.

At the bridesmaids' party, you may present your thank-you gifts to your attendants and flower girl. If you are giving special gifts to your wedding party at this time, you may not want to include anyone other than attendants and very close relatives on the gift list. A gift for your mother and the groom's mother may also be presented now. If other family and friends are invited, you may wish to save the gifts until the rehearsal dinner.

Your gifts for your attendants should be permanent items of a personal nature that somehow relate to this special day. All bridesmaids should receive the same gift with the maid- or matron-of-honor receiving something a little more special. If either of your children are involved, you may also wish to single them out with a gift that is "a little more sentimental" than the others.

An alternative approach to the bridesmaids' party is a "bachelorette" party—one last outing for you as a "single" woman. If you prefer this type of party, it is usually hosted by your maid- or matron-of-honor. You may not feel comfortable inviting your mother, your future mother-in-law, or the children to this type of party, and it should be held several days before the wedding. You will have the rehearsal dinner the night before the wedding, and you do not want to be "partied out" so that you cannot enjoy the big day itself.

The Bachelor Party

This is the pre-wedding party that is most steeped in tradition, and this is as true for second marriages as it is for first-time grooms. Unlike tradition, bachelor parties of today are becoming a gathering or a re-union of old friends whose purpose is to celebrate, reminisce, and wish the groom well.

Customarily, the bachelor party was held the night before the wedding, but it is becoming much more accepted to have this night-of-nights the weekend before the wedding. This gives plenty of time to recuperate and allows for the wedding rehearsal to be the night before the wedding.

The party is usually hosted by the best man, but it can be thrown by relatives, male family members, close friends, or the groom. Generally, all male members of the wedding party are invited, along with other close friends and family. Both fathers and all sons from a previous marriage can be included on the invitation list, but if they do attend, they will probably only stay for a short time.

The bachelor party may be the time the groom chooses to give his gifts to his groomsmen. If, however, the evening's activities are planned to be on the "wild" side, he will want to synchronize his gift giving with you and choose the rehearsal dinner as a better time. Such gifts should be similar to your attendants' gifts and should be personal and lasting in nature.

If you are concerned about the traditional activities that are said to occur at some bachelor parties, you should feel free to talk openly with your fiancé about any concerns you may have about the party activities that may have been planned. Make certain that if drinking of alcoholic beverages will be part of the bachelor party, arrangements have been made by the host for safe rides home or for designated drivers.

Today, many couples whose friends are single or whose friends are from different locations are combining the bachelor and bachelorette parties into one celebration. It is a perfect time for attendants, groomsmen, and other friends to form new friendships of their own.

The Rehearsal Dinner

This dinner, or party of some sort, almost always follows the wedding rehearsal, which is generally held the evening before the wedding. Even when a small wedding does not require a rehearsal, an intimate dinner on the eve of the ceremony is a friendly way to let members of each family get to know one another.

The groom's parents customarily host the rehearsal dinner, but if he is older, and especially if this is his second marriage, he may wish to host the party himself.

Everyone who participates in the wedding rehearsal and their spouse should be invited to the rehearsal dinner—attendants, clergy, parents, grandparents, parents of children involved in the wedding, out-of-town guests who have arrived, as well as other close friends and relatives. It is up to you and the groom to decide for certain whether or not to include dates, spouses, and, if applicable, divorced parents. If all of the extended families are cordial, it is usually customary to invite both parents and stepparents.

A rehearsal dinner can range from a formal sit-down dinner with white linen tablecloths to an outdoor barbecue or dessert buffet. A seated dinner that is more understated than the wedding with simpler food, drink, and decor is still the most popular choice, but it can be an expensive one. If the groom is hosting the rehearsal dinner, because of his many other financial obligations, it is better to have a less formal evening and include everyone and their spouses than it is to have a nicer event for just those included in the wedding party.

Depending on the length of time between the engagement announcement and the wedding, the rehearsal and the rehearsal dinner invitations should be sent from three weeks to ten days ahead of time. This guarantees that there will be no question as to who is invited, when it begins, and how long the evening will last. If the rehearsal dinner is to be formal, engraved invitations should be ordered and issued. A formal invitation for a rehearsal dinner hosted by the groom may read as follows:

The pleasure of your company is requested
at the Rehearsal Dinner for
Susan Sumner and Ken Buehler
on Saturday, the 11th day of June
at seven o'clock P.M.
Ogden Golf and Country Club
Ogden, Utah

R.S.V.P.

Mr. Ken Buehler
2800 Fillmore
Ogden, Utah 84403

Response cards should be printed and included with all formal invitations. A response card might read as follows:

Please respond on or before May 25, 1995

*M*______________________________

will attend rehearsal

*M*______________________________

will attend rehearsal dinner

Number of persons for dinner ________

An informal rehearsal dinner invitation can be issued on purchased notes with an R.S.V.P. by telephone.

In the instance where the groom is hosting the dinner, you may wish to have all R.S.V.P.'s sent or telephoned directly to you, causing less stress for the groom!

Toasts are historic at the rehearsal dinner. First, there is the customary salute to the couple by the best man. If the groom's son is not the best man, yet is old enough and he feels comfortable doing so, you may prefer to have him make the first toast. The groom then follows with a toast to the bride and his new family (or in-laws, if there are no children). Then the bride toasts the groom and his children (or in-laws, if there are no children). Attendants might also want to toast. From there, other guests propose toasts that include anecdotes about the bride and groom. If, however, the toasts go on too long, your fiancé should be prepared with a wrap-up thought to bring the evening to a close and get everyone home early enough to feel rested and relaxed for the wedding itself.

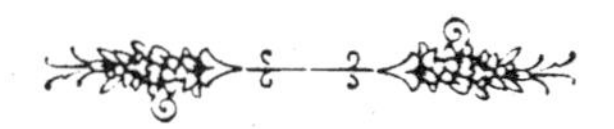

"The web (of marriage) is fashioned of love. Yes, but many kinds of love: romantic love first, then slow-growing devotion, and playing through these, a constantly rippling relationship. It is made of loyalties and interdependencies and shared experiences. It is woven of memories of meeting and conflicts; of triumphs and disappointments. It is a web of communication, a common language, and the acceptance of lack of language, too."

—Anne Morrow Lindbergh

INVITATIONS

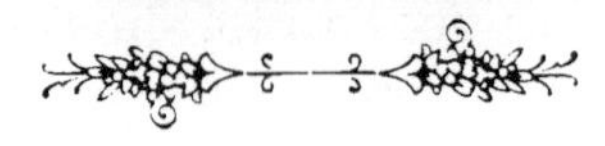

From the first announcement of your engagement to family and friends to the final thank-you notes sent to all of those who shared in your special day, the wedding stationery you select—the type of paper, the kind of engraving, the style of writing, and the font for the lettering—is indicative of the style and the formality of the wedding festivities that are to be given for and by you.

Tradition has established guidelines for which stationery is appropriate for every style of wedding, and these guidelines are as true for second marriages as they are for firsts. Which is the one you will choose? Heavy, white paper and the finest engraving for a very formal wedding? A more informal handwritten, calligraphic note on rose-colored paper for a garden wedding? White paper printed in gold, rolled into a tube that is tied with ribbon and filled with confetti, for a contemporary affair?

Whichever you select, you can be creative, within the consistency of style and formality. Basically, there are two categories of stationery that you will use:

1. The formal or informal pieces to be used

for shower/party invitations, written invitations, printed mementos, and thank-you notes.

2. The formal or informal invitations and enclosures asking guests to the ceremony and/or reception and/or the announcements declaring that the marriage has taken place.

The amount of time between the announcement of the engagement and the wedding date will dictate when the wedding invitations should be ordered. If there is several months' time, you will want to order the invitations at least four months prior to the wedding. If not, order the invitations immediately after deciding on a date and a location. Plan on three to four weeks for the stationer to fill your order for printed material, but make certain you ask for an exact time from order date to delivery date. Depending on your pre-wedding schedule and number of invited guests, allow a minimum of two weeks to address and mail the wedding invitations (longer if you are using a calligrapher). The invitations should be mailed four to six weeks prior to the wedding.

Who is invited to the wedding is a decision that you and the groom will need to agree on as quickly as possible. It is something that needs to be discussed openly so that there are no hard feelings or misunderstandings. The two of you need to agree on a budget and a maximum number of guests, which may be restricted by the site you have selected.

Order one invitation for each married or co-habitating couple that you plan to invite. The officiant and spouse, the attendants, the groomsmen, and all helpers should also receive an invitation. It is not necessary to invite dates of single guests with a separate invitation.

Always order extras of everything. One calculation is approximately 25 percent more than your actual count. This may seem excessive, but it is much less expensive to order all at once and have a few extra than to place a very small order because you need just five more! Mistakes will be made, guests will be added at the last minute, and you will receive several requests for extras that are going to be kept as mementos.

There are traditional guidelines on the wording of invitations which may be used when deciding on the phrasing for your wedding invitations (these are explained in detail in *Wedding Stationery: Perfect Invitations, Enclosures, Thank Yous, and More* by Jo

Packham). In the case of most second marriages, however, you and the groom host your own wedding, so a typical invitation might read as follows:

Ms. Heidi Glassman
and
Mr. Douglas Kemp
request the honour of your presence
at their marriage
Saturday, the fifth of December
at seven o'clock in the evening
Nineteen hundred and ninety-three
Lake Shore Country Club
Laguna Beach

If you wish to include your children's names on the invitation, it may read as follows:

Ms. Heidi Glassman
with her daughter Sara Glassman
and
Mr. Douglas Kemp
with his son Michael Kemp
request the honour of your presence
at the union of their families
Saturday, the fifth of December
at seven o'clock in the evening
Nineteen hundred and ninety-three
Lake Shore Country Club
Laguna Beach

If you have been married before and your parents are hosting your second wedding, the invitation may read as follows:

Mr. and Mrs. Stephen John Thompson
request the honour of your presence
at the marriage of their daughter
Mrs. Sarah Thompson Glazier
to
Mr. Allan David Shaw
Friday, the first of August
at seven o'clock in the evening
Nineteen hundred and ninety-three
The Hermitage
Providence, Rhode Island

If you are older and are getting remarried, and if the married children of yours and the groom are hosting the wedding, the children should be listed alphabetically:

Mr. and Mrs. Michael William Bingham
Mr. and Mrs. James Andrew Freemont
Mr. and Mrs. Daniel Spencer Wood
request the honour of your presence
at the marriage of their parents
Ms. Mary Hawkings Wood
and
Mr. David Andrew Freemont
Friday, the fifteenth of November
at six o'clock in the evening
Nineteen hundred and ninety-three
First Baptist Church
Greenville, South Carolina

If you are planning a very small wedding and/or reception, wedding announcements are primarily used. Because this is your second marriage, they will probably be sent by you and the groom. Their purpose is to inform family and friends from out of town, those you have not seen for a while but still feel a kinship with, and all others you would like to have invited to the wedding but were unable to because of size restrictions.

One way of wording an announcement made by you and the groom is as follows:

Ms. Jennifer Ann MacCarthy
and
Mr. Daniel Buehler
have the pleasure of announcing
their marriage
on Saturday, the fifteenth of August
One thousand nine hundred and ninety-three
Jackson Hole, Wyoming

If you wish to include the children's names, the announcement might read as follows:

Ms. Jennifer Ann MacCarthy
with her daughter Sandra MacCarthy
and Mr. Daniel Buehler
with his son Joshua Buehler
have the pleasure of announcing
the joining of their two families
on Saturday, the fifteenth of August
One thousand nine hundred and ninety-three
Jackson Hole, Wyoming

WEDDING CEREMONY STYLE

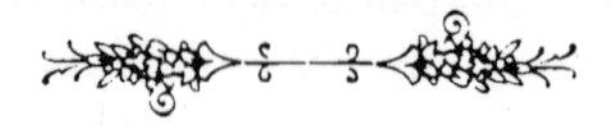

"Somewhere in the chain, sometimes placed early in the succession of links, sometimes later, is the wedding ceremony."

Your wedding day is probably one of the most important days of your life, one of the richest experiences you and your beloved will ever share. You may want your ceremony to be laced with tradition or you may choose one that is more contemporary in nature. Whichever you choose, to ensure that you will have the ceremony that is "perfect" in your eyes, you will want to plan carefully and discuss openly with your fiancé every aspect of the wedding ceremony itself. The two of you will want to decide exactly what type of ceremony you want, the significance of the vows you will recite, any individual changes or additions you would like, and what each of you feels is important for the ceremony to express about yourselves, your families, your beliefs, and the marriage you have planned together.

One very important issue in regard to the wedding ceremony is whether or not it will be representative of one particular faith. If you have both worshipped in the same place for an extended period of time, then choosing the person to perform the ceremony and the place to exchange vows will be easy. For couples who have moved, have been inactive in their faith, who have no specified religious affiliation, or who both have equally strong, but different, religious convictions, this choice can be extremely difficult. With a second marriage, you may also face the obstacles placed before you by certain religions that have doctrine dictating the circumstances and procedures for second marriages.

After discussing this issue completely and honestly with your fiancé, you will need to decide on what type of ceremony, who will perform the ceremony, and where you wish to have it held. Contact and meet with the official or officials you wish to have perform the ceremony as soon as possible. Have a list of questions and requests so that nothing will be forgotten and there will be no surprises. Discuss the issue of second marriages as it relates to the church officiant, as well as the music, prayers, scriptures, vows, and so on. Be certain to take care of any misunderstandings, misconceptions, and uncertainties before the wedding. Do not wait until the ceremony has begun or the wedding is over to voice an opinion or grievance.

If you are planning on a religious service and wish to include children from a former marriage, you will want to discuss these desires with the church officiant. Such circumstances are the exception, rather than the norm, and special considerations and permissions may have to be obtained.

Choose the style of ceremony that reflects the feelings, desires, and beliefs of both you and the groom. If that is a traditional religious ceremony, then the circumstances are somewhat dictated by the officiant, but if it is any variation on this theme, the two of you should express your desires and make certain they are incorporated into the entire wedding plans. Ceremony styles include:

Formal:

Steeped in tradition and laced with all of the pageantry and finery the occasion has to offer is the formal wedding. The ceremony is eloquent and religious, the wedding party is extensive, the gowns are grand, the men are dressed in tails, there are limousines to deliver the bride and her escort to the church and to drive off with the groom and his newly beloved, and the reception that follows is truly an event to remember.

Certain publications on wedding etiquette state that it is improper to have a traditional formal wedding for a second marriage. I feel, however, that if for one reason or another this is what you and the groom have decided upon, then it is indeed appropriate. If one of you has never been married before, and a large, traditional, formal wedding is what you want, then it is what you should have. Oftentimes, brides who are having a large formal wedding for their second marriage will change tradition slightly and wear a cream-colored wedding gown without a train or have their son or a close friend give them away at the altar.

Semiformal:

Most formal wedding procedures also apply to the smaller, semiformal wedding—they are simply done on a less lavish scale. You will have fewer guests and attendants.

Informal:

An intimate, informal wedding can be held anywhere from a small chapel to your home. Guests are welcomed and directed by a member of the wedding party who is familiar with almost everyone who is invited. You and the groom (and the children) will probably mingle before the ceremony. At ceremony time, the two of you, your maid- or matron-of-honor, and the best man take your places before the ceremony officiant. After the ceremony and the traditional kiss, the two of you simply turn to receive congratulations from the guests.

	Very Formal	Formal	Semiformal	Informal
Style	Traditional expensive, elaborate	More relaxed, most popular	Between formal and informal	Whatever you desire
Invitations/Announcements	Engraved on heavy, white or ivory paper; card folded; two envelopes; enclosures	Engraved or printed on heavy, white or ivory paper; single or folded card—one or two envelopes; enclosures	Printed on any color paper, additions such as photo-graphs; one envelope	Printed, handwritten on any color paper or style that is appropriate is acceptable
Ceremony	Church, synagogue, temple, ballroom	Church, synagogue, temple, ballroom, home, country club	Anywhere that is appropriate	Anywhere desired
Reception	Large, lavish dinner and music	Dinner and music	Usually includes meal, maybe music	Small and simple
Food/Beverages	Champagne, wine or liquor and assorted beverages Sit-down or large buffet, bridal party and guests have tables	Champagne or punch, other drinks optional Buffet, bridal party may have tables	Champagne for toasts, other drinks optional Stand-up buffet	Champagne for toasts, tea, coffee, other drinks optional Snacks or cake

	Very Formal	*Formal*	*Semiformal*	*Informal*
Decorations/Accessories	Elaborate flowers for church and reception Canopy, pew ribbons, aisle carpet, limousines, groom's cake, engraved napkins	Flowers for church and reception Limousines and other items optional	Flowers for altar, some decorations for reception	Whatever you desire
Music	Organ at church, soloist optional, dancing at reception	Organ at church, soloist optional, dancing optional	Organ at church	Usually no music
Guest List	Over 200 guests	75-200 guests	Under 100 guests	Not more than 50 guests
Bride	Elegant, long dress, long sleeves/ gloves, long train, veil	Long dress, any sleeve length, veil, shorter train	Morning wedding—knee length Evening—floor length, veil/hat/ wreath	Dress or suit or whatever you desire
Females	6-8 attendants, long dress	2-6 attendants, long dress	1-3 attendants, dress based on length, style of bride's	1 attendant, dress or suit or casual
Males	Cutaway long jacket or stroller for day; tailcoat for night	Cutaway stroller or tuxedo for day; tuxedo for night	Stroller, tuxedo, dinner jacket for day; tuxedo, dinner jacket, suit, or blazer for evening	Business suit, blazer

Religious:

Personal preference and the religious beliefs of you and your fiancé will determine the type of religious wedding ceremony that you will have. If you are of one faith, the decision is easy. If you are of different denominations, you may agree on one ceremony, try to combine ideas from both, or write your own. The important thing is that you discuss the matter with each other and with the wedding officiant, and that each of you is in agreement with the final decision.

Ecumenical -- Interfaith:

Each church or temple may have different requirements and procedures in an interfaith second marriage ceremony, so it is important to discuss the requirements with the officiants of both. The ceremonies are usually held on neutral grounds, but in certain circumstances, clergy members will allow interfaith weddings to take place in one or the other church or temple. Usually a clergyman from both officiates during the ceremony. You will both have to meet with both clergymen at the same time to discuss the ceremony procedures and guidelines.

Nondenominational:

This ceremony is usually similar to the traditional Protestant ceremony and possesses the flexibility for you to write part of your own vows. Its purpose is to allow you to be married with a spiritual essence without the structure and restrictions of established traditional religions. The ceremony can be offered by the Unitarian church or other nondenominational groups.

Civil:

Most civil marriages are performed in a courthouse, a judge's chambers, the home of the justice of the peace, or at city hall. They are quiet, intimate, fast, easy, and economical, and they require only a marriage license. They can be performed by a variety of officials. Laws on who can marry you vary from state to state, so be certain to check with your marriage license bureau to find out what your state specifies.

Traditional:

The traditional wedding usually takes place in a church or temple and is performed by a clergy member of a religious faith. There are many variations based on the traditions and restrictions placed by the clergy member and the religion.

Nontraditional:

Some couples think the taking of vows in a church or hotel with any type of tradition attached is entirely too mainstream for their wants or needs. They prefer an event that is associated with what they love to do together the most. Those who love to ski can be married on the slopes, scuba-divers can be married underwater, or if either of you are avid baseball players, you could be married on home plate. Whatever it is that you want is exactly the way the nontraditional ceremony should be handled.

If you prefer a nontraditional wedding, but do not care to go to the extremes of being married underwater, then a wedding that is considered contemporary in nature may take place in a lodge in the middle of the redwoods, at a historical site, or overlooking the ocean. Home garden weddings or resort weddings are also considered nontraditional, but they are becoming extremely popular in today's society.

Regardless of which ceremony style you finally decide upon, you will want to make certain that you discuss everything in detail with your fiancé and that you approach this affair with some type of organizational chart. Make sure you allow yourself ample time to make all of the arrangements.

On the following pages is a Ceremony Checklist that may be of some help with all of your planning.

Ceremony Checklist

Officiant ______________________________

Phone ______________________________

Officiant Fee ______________________________

Location of Ceremony ______________________________

Address ______________________________

Phone ______________________________

Person in Charge of Location ______________________________

Fee ______________________________

Transportation ______________________________

Person in Charge
of Transportation ______________________________

Arrival Time ______________________________

Where to Dress ______________________________

Time to Begin ______________________________

Opening Words by ______________________________

Readings by ______________________________

____

____

Prayers Given by ______________________

____

____

____

Changes in
Marriage Vows ________________________

____

____

____

____

Music ________________________________

Organist ______________________________

Soloists ______________________________

Musicians _____________________________

Closing Words by ______________________

Time to End ___________________________

Rehearsal Date _________________________

Time _________________________________

Rehearsal Coordinator __________________

Phone ______________________________

Guest Book / Pen ______________________

Person in Charge ______________________

Wedding Programs ____________________

Person in Charge ______________________

Reserved Seating / Bride ______________

Names / Pew 1 _______________________

Names / Pew 2 _______________________

Names / Pew 3 _______________________

Usher in Charge _______________________

Reserved Seating / Groom _____________

Names / Pew 1 _______________________

Names / Pew 2 _______________________

Names / Pew 3 _______________________

Usher in Charge _______________________

Person to
Accept Gifts __________________________

Servers _____________________________

____

Person in Charge ______________________

Phone ______________________________

Rice / Flower Petals ___________________

Person in Charge ______________________

Janitor ______________________________

Janitor Fees __________________________

Parking Availability ____________________

Parking Attendants _____________________

Photo Session _________________________

Photographer _________________________

Location _____________________________

Time ________________________________

Marriage License _______________________

Bride's Phone __________________________

Groom's Phone _________________________

Wedding Coordinator ___________________

Phone _______________________________

Notes ________________________________

Ceremony Sites

Once you have decided on your wedding style, you will need to select the location. Begin your search for a ceremony site as soon as you have selected the date for your wedding. Select a site that is appropriate for the style of wedding you have chosen and remember that any sight is appropriate for a second marriage ceremony if it is what you want. If you plan your ceremony to take place in a location other than a church or temple, keep in mind the preparations you may have to orchestrate. Consider all of the details, including such issues as how accessible the site is, what facilities exist for guest parking and seating, and what equipment is available. If it is to be outdoors, remember to select an alternate location in case the weather is bad.

Ceremony Site Checklist

Type of Ceremony ______________________

Date ______________________________

Time ______________________________

Location ___________________________

Address ___________________________

Person in Charge ______________________

Phone Number ______________________

Clergy/Officiant ______________________

Phone Number ______________________

Minimum Guests ______________________

Maximum Guests ______________________

Length of Time Available ________________

Earliest Arrival Time __________________

Departure Time ______________________

Fees/Due Date ______________________

Dressing Rooms ______________________

Number ___________________________

Time Available ______________________

Rehearsal Time ______________________

Floral Arrangements Set-up Time ________

Photography Rules and Restrictions _______

Photography Set-up Time ________________

Audio Equipment/Cost ________________

Gift Table ________________________________

Equipment / Costs:

Runner ________________________________

Aisle Stanchions ________________________

Kneeling Bench ________________________

Wedding Altar __________________________

Wedding Arch __________________________

Candleabras ____________________________

Candles ________________________________

Chairs ________________________________

Guest Book Table ______________________

Misc. ________________________________

____

____

____

Person in Charge:

Removal of Flowers
to Reception Site ____________________

Other ____________________

Coat/Hat Room Attendant ____________

Fees Due/Date ____________________

Janitor ____________________

Janitor Fees ____________________

Parking Availability ________________

Parking Attendants ________________

Notes ____________________

____

____

____

____

____

____

____

____

The Ceremony Rehearsal

Your wedding ceremony is one of the most important events the two of you will ever share. To make certain your ceremony is everything you want it to be, you must be organized from the beginning and you must plan a rehearsal to give yourself and the entire wedding party a chance to practice each part, answer each question, and attend to last-minute details.

Discuss all of your ceremony plans at a pre-marriage conference held with the officiant, you, the groom, and the wedding consultant, if appropriate. The time to discuss the details and ask any questions is at this meeting and not at the actual rehearsal when everyone else is present. If you take the time to go over your plans with parents, attendants, and the clergy ahead of time, there will be no surprises or hurt feelings.

1. The presence of every member of the actual wedding party is of the utmost importance at the rehearsal. However, discourage wedding party spouses and friends from attending the actual rehearsal, and invite them to the rehearsal dinner or party afterward. Include the bridal consultant, if one is being employed. It is a nice idea to invite out-of-town guests who have traveled a considerable distance to also attend the rehearsal dinner, but not the rehearsal.

2. It is a good idea to send out written invitations to those you want to be at the rehearsal ceremony and dinner.

3. The wedding rehearsal should be scheduled to allow at least two hours. It should be scheduled shortly before the wedding and be conducted in the location where the ceremony is to be performed.

4. Traditionally, the rehearsal takes place the night before the wedding with a rehearsal dinner for participants following. However, it is appropriate to hold it up to five days before the festivities.

5. Take pictures at the rehearsal. These are memories that will last a lifetime, and, because you are so nervous or busy, you may not get to see everything that happens.

6. The organist and members of the church staff who are assisting with the ceremony must also be present at the rehearsal. These participants should be notified by you, the person placed in charge of the rehearsal, or the church secretary.

7. Remind each participant to dress appropriately. The type of dinner or the church (or temple) itself may impose restrictions on attire.

8. The bridal consultant should also be notified of the time and date of the rehearsal and should be present to offer needed services, but should in no way interfere with the conduct of the rehearsal.

9. For a religious ceremony, the minister or rabbi will be the determining factor in certain aspects of the ceremony. This person is the only one who can give instructions as to how the ceremony must be conducted, as he/she is the only one who knows and understands the rules by which he/she is governed.

10. For a civil ceremony, you and the groom can decide on the procedure of the ceremony. This is your day and you should be allowed to state how it will proceed. If, however, you are unsure as to what to do in exactly what order, the traditional guidelines outlined in *Wedding Ceremonies: Planning Your Special Day* by Jo Packham will help in making your decision.

11. The marriage service will not be read in full at the rehearsal, so go over any special requests or variations needed to understand the exact order of events and to outline the roles of the wedding party involved. All participants, whether taking pictures or performing a musical selection, should do an actual run through of their parts. Practice will help reinforce understanding of their roles so that there will be no mistakes. You may want to be as detailed as bringing stand-in bouquets, the rings, the ring bearer's cushion, and other props, so that everyone can practice his/her part.

12. Practice passing the bouquet. After you reach the altar, your maid- or matron-of-honor will pass her bouquet to the next in line so that she can adjust your gown. You can either pass her your bouquet now so that your hands will be free during the ceremony or you can wait until the exchange of the rings to give her your flowers. At the end of the ceremony, your maid- or matron-of-honor hands back your bouquet, adjusts your gown, and you begin the recessional.

13. Practice exchanging the rings. The best man or the ring bearer holds the rings during the ceremony. At the appropriate time, the best man produces the rings, either from his pocket or from the cushion, and hands them to the clergy member. The clergy member hands the bride's ring to the groom with his palms up. This will eliminate the possibility of the ring being dropped during the handing off. He does the same for the bride.

14. Make certain the photographer knows when it is and is not appropriate to take pictures during the ceremony. Also, arrange with him for the required pictures immediately before and after the ceremony. A very specific list may save confusion and disappointment.

15. Before the rehearsal is over, repeat all of the instructions, times, and places with each participant individually. Give each person a checklist. Let each person explain to you individually what his/her responsibilities are so that there are no misunderstandings. Ask if there are any questions and answer them immediately.

16. Have the officiant check the marriage license and make certain the witnesses have been notified and have given their consent to signing on your behalf.

17. A rehearsal for a ceremony of any size is reassuring for everyone involved, but some clergy members or civil officials do not schedule one for small ceremonies or those being held in public places. In that case, everyone should assemble an hour or two before the ceremony so that brief instructions can be given in advance.

Processional:

The ushers walk up the aisle in pairs, starting with shortest to tallest. The bridesmaids follow (in pairs if there are more than four, or singly if you choose), also starting with the shortest. If there is an uneven number and you wish them to walk in pairs, the first attendant may walk in singly. The maid- or matron-of-honor is next, followed by the ring bearer and flower girl. The ring bearer can walk either before or with the flower girl.

The organist pauses again for a moment to indicate that you and your escort are about to enter. The music begins and you slowly walk down the aisle. The guests rise until the officiant asks them to be seated (the procession for a Catholic wedding follows the same procedures, except that the bride is not given away; her escort walks her to the steps of the altar, where her groom and the church officiant are waiting). The escort then places your hand in the groom's hand. He may kiss you before taking his seat on the first row.

At the Altar:

The officiant stands at the altar, facing the guests, with you on the left and the groom on the right. The best man stands next to the groom, the ring bearer is next, and then the ushers. The maid- or matron-of-honor stands next to you and the flower girl stands next to her. The bridesmaids line up next to the flower girl.

To be certain everyone is standing in the right position, you might want to place a penny or a flower petal on the spot where each attendant is to stand. This will avoid crowding.

Recessional:

Upon completion of the ceremony, the organist plays as you and the groom walk arm-in-arm down the aisle. The flower girl and ring bearer pair off and follow behind. Then the maid- or matron-of-honor and the best man pair off, followed by pairs of the bridesmaids and ushers. The officiant follows the last bridesmaid and usher. You may want to form a receiving line immediately after the ceremony. Your guests will want to give their congratulations as soon as possible. After the recessional, the ushers return to the ceremony site and escort guests out.

Receiving Line -- For All Ceremonies:

Procedures that are appropriate for your particular ceremony and circumstances should be followed upon completion of the recessional.

The receiving line should be formed in the vestibule of the church or temple, if the clergy permits, or in an area close to, but away from, the altar. You may want to consider having only you and the groom, and the older children from both marriages (if they agree to stand and meet all of those strangers) in this receiving line. If there is to be a receiving line at the reception, then all of the attendants may or may not join you at that time. Regardless of your choice, be sure the people you expect to join you are told at the rehearsal. Now family and friends may file through the line offering their best wishes and congratulations.

At informal weddings today, some brides elect not to have a wedding line. To make it easier on your guests, you will want to be certain to station yourself and the groom in a place that is obvious and accessible.

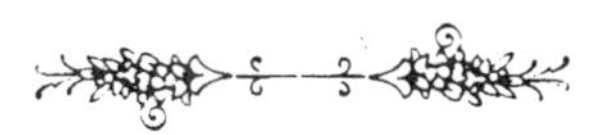

"Never forget that both of you have the spark of the divine in you. Whatever you do or do not do won't change that fact."
—Elaine Cannon

WEDDING RECEPTION STYLE

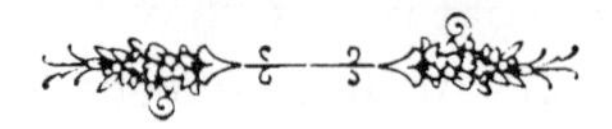

The reception is usually the event that is shared by the largest number of guests and the memorable finale to one of the most important days of your life. The style of the reception was decided upon when the style for the ceremony was chosen.

Thorough and careful planning are needed to ensure results that you so desire. Whether you are orchestrating a large, formal affair for 500, or conducting a small garden ceremony and reception intended to be shared only with those closest to you, you will need to make the same decisions for your second reception as you did for the first—decisions about style, location, flowers, the wedding cake, and much, much more.

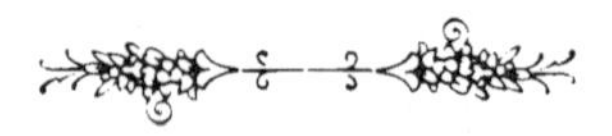

"This is a wonderful world. The richness, the hope, the promise of life today, are exciting beyond belief. Nonetheless, we need stout hearts and strong characters; we need knowledge and training, we need organized effort to meet the future."

—Belle S. Spafford

Reception Sites

Next, you want to select a location for the reception. Begin your search for a reception site as soon as you have selected the date of your wedding and the site for the ceremony. When you plan the location, keep in mind the preparations you may have to orchestrate. Consider all of the details, including how accessible the site is, what facilities exist for guest parking and seating, and what equipment is available. Some of your options are hotels, clubs, restaurants, reception centers, at home, or out-of-doors.

Depending on the location of the reception and what its "package" includes, you may have to make decisions on the following:

1. A wedding coordinator.

2. The caterer.

3. Seating at the reception.

a. The bride's table.

This table can be of any shape and can be placed wherever in the room that is most strategic (at the end of a long room, the middle of the room, or on an elevated platform) for all guests to see you and the groom. Unless the table is round, seating is on one side only so that the guests' views are not obstructed. You and the groom sit in the center of the table; your honor attendant sits on the groom's left, with the best man seated on your right, unless you opt to place either the groom's or your children in these places of honor. The bridesmaids and ushers are then alternated around the table. Attendants who are married to each other sit together.

b. Special children's table.

If you have included several young children on your guest list, it is often nice to have a special table with a specific chaperon for them. You may wish to include additional items, such as coloring books, for them to entertain themselves while the adults have a leisurely meal.

4. The wedding cake.

5. Reception flowers.

6. Decorations for the reception site.

Finances

Additional decisions that will need to be made by you and the groom are how the wedding festivities will be financed. Because this is your second marriage, you are wiser about the true costs of a wedding and probably in a position to pay for the wedding yourselves. Because such an investment will affect the finances of you and your new husband in the beginning, it is important that the two of you talk openly and honestly about financing. If the events become a financial strain on either of you, it will be remembered as exactly that. What you need to understand and remember is that with a little creativity and a lot of planning, your wedding can be a most beautiful and memorable event—regardless of how much money was spent.

Traditionally, you and your family pay for most of the wedding costs. Today, however, with long-distance weddings, divorced parents, second marriages, and uneven guest lists, many rules and roles have changed. I have listed the traditional guidelines of who pays for what. You may wish to take these guidelines and adapt them to meet your specific needs. Because you are getting married for the second time, you and the groom may choose to finance the entire wedding yourselves with families helping in a small way, such as paying for the rehearsal dinner or perhaps the flowers. If you and the groom have decided to finance the wedding yourselves, the two of you will need to decide how much and which one of you will pay for what. You might divide the costs directly down the middle or divide them down more traditional lines with you taking your family's responsibilities and the groom taking his. The most important point is that you and your fiancé agree on the decisions that are made and that the amounts decided upon are reasonable.

Traditionally, you and your family pay for the following:

1. The engagement party, if you host it.

2. The invitations, announcements, enclosure cards, personal stationery, and thank-you notes, including stamps for mailing.

3. Your wedding dress, veil, and accessories.

4. Your trousseau of clothes and lingerie.

5. The bride's parents' wedding attire and the attire required for any family members still living at home.

6. The groom's ring.

7. A wedding gift for you and the groom.

8. Gifts for the attendants.

9. All hotel accommodations for your out-of-town attendants.
10. Any bridal consultant fees.
11. All expenses of the ceremony, except for those specified as the groom's family expenses (see page 74), including rental fee for the church or ceremony site and fees for any additional equipment such as aisle carpets or candle holders.
12. Fees for all wedding participants (other than family members, friends, or relatives), such as the organist or soloist, but not including the ceremony official.
13. All expenses of the reception:

- **a.** Rental fee for the reception site.
- **b.** All food and beverage charges.
- **c.** All catering charges.
- **d.** The wedding cake or cakes.
- **e.** Music for the reception.
- **f.** Fees for such items as guest book or wedding register.
- **g.** Fees for additional equipment.
- **h.** Fees for additional help.

14. The following flowers:

- **a.** All flowers used for decorating the ceremony and reception sites.

b. Bouquets or corsages for the bridesmaids, honor attendants, and flower girl.

c. Flowers or corsages for any other wedding participants in addition to the wedding party.

d. Corsages or flowers given to any special relatives or friends who may have helped.

e. Flowers sent to any hostess who entertained for you or for you and the groom before your wedding day.

15. Your photograph taken before the ceremony.

16. All photography and any recordings or videotaping of the ceremony or reception.

17. All charges for transporting the bridal party to the wedding site and from there to the reception site.

18. All expenses involved in parking cars, security, and traffic control.

Traditionally, the groom and his family pay for the following:

1. Your engagement and wedding rings.

2. A wedding gift for you and the groom.

3. The marriage license.

4. The groom's parents' personal wedding attire and accessories.

5. Gloves, ties, and ascots for all men in the wedding party.

6. Hotel accommodations for the groom's out-of-town groomsmen.

7. Gifts for the best man and out-of-town groomsmen.

8. The rehearsal dinner.

9. Ceremony official's fee.

10. Your flowers, including going-away corsage and throwing bouquet.

11. Groom's boutonniere and those for his groomsmen.

12. Corsages for mothers and grandmothers.

13. Complete honeymoon trip.

Planning the Reception

After you and the groom have decided upon the style of your wedding and agreed on the financing and budget for the entire affair, you can begin the planning of your festivities. Careful and detailed planning can ensure the "perfect" wedding reception. If you are planning a small affair with fewer than a hundred guests, you and your attendants can probably do all of the planning yourselves. If you intend to have a large, formal affair, you may need professional help from a wedding coordinator.

Remember to include the groom in any major decisions concerning the wedding festivities. And, if there are children involved, it is always nice to ask their opinion. Getting their advice cannot only be a major help, but it can also make both the groom and the children feel involved and get your marriage off on a positive note of communicating and sharing.

You will need to consider the time of day you want your reception. Your choice may be determined by your religious beliefs, by the availability of the site, by the formality of the occasion, and by where you live. The time of your reception dictates, to a certain extent, what type of reception it will be.

The traditional types are:

a. A morning breakfast or brunch.

b. An afternoon luncheon, tea, or cocktail party.

c. An evening dinner, buffet, or dessert.

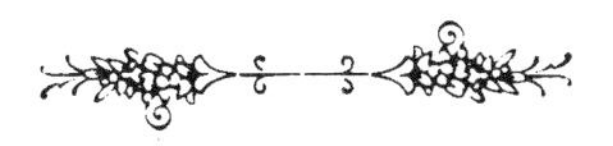

"The best decision I ever made in all my life was to marry my husband at the right time, in the right way, and in the right place."

—Adapted from Virginia Cook Sanders

The guest list is the next step in planning the reception. Certain guests have already been decided upon because they were invited to the showers, parties, and the ceremony. Your wedding style and your budget will dictate how many additional guests you may add to the list. As a general rule, 75% of those invited will actually attend if it is on a weekend or over a holiday; if it takes place during the week or during the summer months, 60% attendance is probably more realistic.

When deciding on the guest list, in addition to those you both want to include, you and the groom will need to consider the following:

a. How many of your children's friends you are going to allow them to include.

b. Both families' wishes on who they would like to include on the list.

c. Your wedding participants' spouses, escorts, and families.

d. Your policy on inviting guests' children.

e. Your decision on inviting out-of-town guests.

PLANNING YOUR CALENDAR

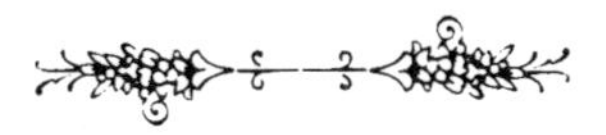

This is one of the most important steps in your plans for the reception. There are so many details to remember, a calender will help you to prioritize the many responsibilities associated with planning a reception. The calender for your second wedding will probably read the same as it did for the first ceremony and reception that was planned. The only differences will occur due to a difference in size, style, and the time between the engagement and the wedding date.

Six Months Before the Wedding:

a. Announce engagement to family and friends as well as in the newspaper.

b. Have engagement party.

c. Decide on style of wedding.

d. Discuss financing with your groom and both families.

e. Plan wedding budget.

f. Decide on size of wedding.

g. Prepare the guest lists:

Bride's.
Bride's family.
Groom's.
Groom's family.

h. Set wedding date and time.

i. Select and invite all wedding party participants:

Honor attendant.
Bridesmaids.
Best man.
Groomsmen and/or ushers.
Flower girl and ring bearer.

j. Consult clergy.

k. Select the wedding coordinator.

l. Select wedding location and make reservations.

m. Select reception location and make reservations.

n. Plan ceremony:

Type of ceremony.
Style of ceremony.
Ceremony vows.
Select ceremony participants.
Decide on music.
Plan the program.
Decide on flowers.
Plan transportation.
Parking.

o. Plan reception:

Cake.
Caterer.
Food.
Liquor.
Servers.
Flowers.

p. Plan rehearsal and rehearsal dinner.

q. Select wedding dress and accessories.

r. Select attire and accessories for attendants.

s. Select attire and accessories for groomsmen.

t. Select attire and accessories for flower girl and ring bearer.

u. Make preliminary reservations for out-of-town guests and wedding participants.

v. Select wedding night suite.

w. Decide on honeymoon:

    Location.
    Travel reservations.
    Hotel accommodations.
    Transportation.

Five Months Before the Wedding:

a. Decide on decorations for the reception, if there are to be any.

b. Select and meet with florist.

c. Select and meet with band/musicians/disc jockey.

d. Select and meet with photographer.

e. Select and meet with videographer.

f. Make final honeymoon plans.

g. Decide on where the two of you will live and begin looking.

h. Meet with stationer and select stationery, enclosures, announcements, and thank-you notes.

Four Months Before the Wedding:

a. Select wedding rings.

b. Finalize ceremony:

    Write and review wedding vows.
    Select special readings and prayers.
    Consult with clergy on ceremony.

c. Set date and time and make reservations for ceremony rehearsal and rehearsal dinner party.

d. Register china, silver, crystal, and gifts with selected stores.

Three Months Before the Wedding:

a. Check final invitation list.

b. Have mothers select gowns, consulting with you and each other.

c. Schedule maid- or matron-of-honor (and bridesmaids, if necessary) to help address all wedding invitations.

d. Address and stamp invitation and announcement envelopes.

e. Schedule attendants' dress and shoe fittings.

f. Schedule physical checkup for you and the groom.

g. Finalize entertainment guide for out-of-town guests.
h. Order wedding accessories, such as ring cushion.
i. Arrange for all rental equipment.
j. Order wedding cake and groom's cake.
k. Make arrangements to have bridal portrait taken.
l. Make final arrangements for transportation.
m. Meet with ceremony and reception musicians and be certain they have music.

Two Months Before the Wedding:

a. Have final fitting for wedding gown.
b. Set date and make reservations for bridesmaids' luncheon.
c. Set date and make reservations for bachelor party.
d. Stuff and mail invitations.
e. Buy attendants' and groomsmen's gifts.
f. Finalize all arrangements in regard to reception.
g. Finalize arrangements with caterer.
h. Finalize orders for flowers.
i. Finalize order for decorations and additional accessories.

j. Finalize arrangements for parking and attendants.
k. Prepare calendars and checklists for ceremony participants.
l. Prepare calendars and checklists for reception participants.
m. Prepare wedding reception agenda.
n. Buy present for the groom (or the bride).
o. Finalize hotel reservations for out-of-town guests and send confirmation letters.
p. Arrange transportation for out-of-town guests.

One Month Before the Wedding:

a. Apply for marriage license.
b. Get blood tests.
c. Have bridal portrait taken.
d. Have florist visit ceremony and reception sites and make all final arrangements.
e. Schedule final fittings for attendants and groomsmen.
f. Mail invitations for rehearsal and rehearsal dinner.
g. Mail invitations for bridesmaids' luncheon.

h. Mail invitations for bachelor dinner.

i. Change insurance policies.

j. Change name and address on driver's license, credit cards and other documents.

k. Write new will and pre-nuptial agreement.

l. Experiment with wedding hairstyle and make-up.

m. Determine seating arrangements for reception and write place cards.

n. Arrange a place for attendants to dress.

o. Prepare, deliver and discuss calendars and checklists for ceremony participants.

p. Prepare, deliver and discuss calendars and checklists for reception participants.

q. Give photographer checklist of wedding photos and calendar, confirming arrangements.

r. Give videographer checklist of events.

s. Give caterer final head count and seating chart, and confirm all other details.

t. Record all gifts and write thank-you notes as they arrive.

u. Finalize transportation arrangements for out-of-town guests.

Two Weeks Before the Wedding:

a. Confirm, review, and coordinate all services one last time:

    Caterer.
    Flowers.
    Photographer.
    Others.

b. Confirm lodging arrangements for out-of-town guests one last time.

c. Have bridesmaids' luncheon.

d. Have bachelor party.

One Week Before the Wedding:

a. Plan a quiet dinner for you and your fiancé.

b. Pack going-away clothing.

c. Pack for honeymoon.

d. Have rehearsal and rehearsal dinner.

e. Deliver announcements to your mother or maid-of-honor to be mailed the day of the wedding.

The Morning of the Wedding:

a. Have your hair done.

b. Make certain that anything that is not being delivered is picked up.

c. You, or someone else, should reconfirm plans with the wedding coordinator, florist, photographer, and musicians.

d. Check to see that the groom has given the ring to the best man.

e. Eat breakfast!!

Two Hours Before the Wedding:

a. Have your attendants arrive at the prearranged location to begin dressing and assist with any last-minute details.

One Hour Before the Wedding:

a. Attendants, parents, groomsmen, and groom should arrive at the ceremony location for pictures or any last-minute details.

Forty-Five Minutes Before the Wedding:

a. The musicians begin playing introductory music.

b. Ushers begin escorting guests to their seats.

Thirty Minutes Before the Wedding:

a. Wedding officiant gives any last-minute instructions to the groom, groomsmen, and/or ushers.

b. Marriage license is given to wedding officiant.

c. Fee is given to wedding officiant by the best man.

d. If the wedding is a formal one, you and your escort leave for the ceremony site at this time.

Ten Minutes Before the Wedding:

a. Wedding party and family go to the vestibule and wait.

b. Ushers escort grandmothers of the bride to their seats.

c. Ushers escort grandmothers of the groom to their seats.

d. Other honored guests are escorted to their seats.

e. For a traditional and formal entrance, you and your escort arrive at the wedding site and join the wedding party.

Five Minutes Before the Wedding:

a. The groom's mother is escorted to her seat, preferably by a member of the groom's family, with her husband following close behind.

b. Any last-minute guests are seated.

c. Your mother is escorted to her seat.

d. The musical solo begins.

One Minute Before the Wedding:

a. Two ushers lay the aisle runner.

Ceremony Time:

a. The officiant takes his position.
b. The groom, accompanied by the best man, enters to the front of the altar.
c. The processional music begins.

One Month Following the Wedding:

a. Write and mail thank-you notes.
b. Return duplicate wedding gifts.

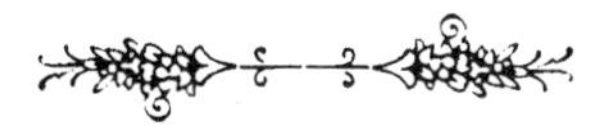

"Two shall be born, the whole wide world apart, and speak in different tongues and have no thought each of the other's being and notice . . . One day out of darkness they shall meet and read life's meaning in each other's eyes."

—Susan Marr Spalding

INDIVIDUALIZING YOUR WEDDING

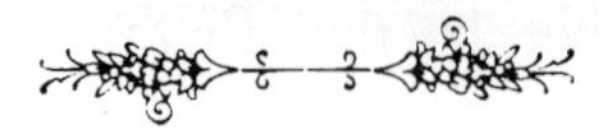

Individualizing your wedding within the bounds of tradition and style makes the event even more meaningful. You, your fiancé, and the children may want to include some of these ideas:

After all of the guests have been seated at the reception, the host traditionally introduces you and the groom by saying something like "May I give to you — for the first time — Mr. and Mrs. Ronald J. Tribe and their children, Mallissa, Samantha, and John." This announcement may be accompanied by a fanfare or drum roll from the band, if you wish. You, the groom, and the children enter from a doorway as the announcement is made or stand if you are seated.

The host then announces the members of the wedding party individually, if seated. Or if the party enters through a doorway, each bridesmaid is escorted by a groomsman and her name is announced first.

The officiant of the wedding ceremony, if he attends, or an honored guest is invited to bless the meal and the couple (or family) as they begin their new life together. This needs to be prearranged so that someone is not called on unexpectedly and is uncomfortable in doing so. This prayer should be in keeping with the religious beliefs of the officiant who performed the ceremony.

Before the meal is about to be served, it is appropriate for the best man to propose a toast to you and the groom. He talks of how you both met and says a few words about the hopes the two of you have for the future. At the end of the toast, he raises his glass and toasts you. All guests raise their glasses and join the toast. You place your arm through the groom's and you both drink. The locking of arms signifies the intertwining of your new lives. He may then make a toast to the children and the union of your two families. The groom may then respond by thanking the best man and toasting the bride, his new family, his new in-laws, and his parents. You then add your own toast honoring the groom, the children, his family, and thanking your parents. (For ideas on what to say, see *Toasts and Speeches* by Jo Packham.)

After you and the groom have finished your meal, the two of you take the dance floor and dance the first dance. The band leader announces the song which has been prearranged because of its special meaning to the two of you.

This dance is traditionally followed by

your dance with your father while the groom dances with your mother; you may, however, wish to each dance with your children. After that, the order is as follows: the groom's father dances with you and the groom with his mother; next you dance with the best man and the groom dances with the maid- or matron-of-honor; then the groom dances with all of the female attendants and you with all of the male attendants; the attendants then dance with each other.

About the time you begin dancing with the best man, the band leader should announce for all of the guests to begin dancing.

After all of the special dances, the cutting of the cake ceremony begins. This is approximately 30 minutes after the meal if there is a formal sit-down dinner with dancing; if not, it is traditional to have this ritual take place approximately one hour after the receiving line ends.

For the cutting of the cake ceremony, you place your hand on the knife and the groom places his hand over yours as the cake is cut. The groom then takes the first piece and feeds part of it to you, after which you do the same. This symbolizes the sharing you will be doing the rest of your lives. A loving gesture that is becoming tradition is for you to give your new in-laws their pieces after that; then the groom serves your parents next. Here again, you may want to serve the children first. The remainder of the cake is then cut and served to the guests.

Another ritual that is a long-standing tradition at weddings is the throwing of the bouquet. You will want to have a smaller bouquet made especially for this moment; that way, the recipient can keep the bouquet as a memento. This usually occurs approximately 30 minutes before your planned departure. The band leader announces the event. All of the unmarried females gather behind you as you toss your bouquet over your shoulder. The person who catches the bouquet is considered lucky and the next to marry.

Next comes the throwing of the garter (this may come before the throwing of the bouquet, if you prefer). As in the bouquet throwing tradition, all of the unmarried males are asked to gather round. You are seated, with the groom standing next to you. With fanfare from the band, he removes your garter and tosses it over his shoulder to the waiting crowd. Oftentimes, the garter is the "something blue" that you have worn to the wedding. The lucky recipient is also the next in line to marry.

With the reception drawing to a close, it is time to make your departure. You will want to retire to the dressing rooms and change into your going-away clothes. You are usually escorted by your mother and bridesmaids. The groom is accompanied by his best man. Of course, here again, the children can be included. As soon as you are ready, you join the groom and have the remaining parents escorted to your room to say your good-byes and thank-yous.

Before you leave, however, you may wish to dance the final farewell dance, at which time all other guests leave the floor. You then make your grand exit with guests throwing rice and extending good wishes as you bring to a close one of the happiest days of your life!

INDEX

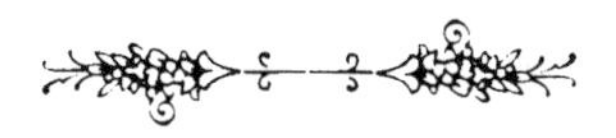